Depth of the River

Vatsala Radhakeesoon

Scarlet Leaf

2017

Vatsala Radhakeesoon   *   *Depth of the River*

SCARLET LEAF PUBLISHING HOUSE

TORONTO ONTARIO CANADA

COPYRIGHT BY VATSALA RADHAKEESOON

ISBN: 978-1-988827-40-7

All rights reserved.

No part of this book can be used or reproduced in any manner whatsoever without written permission, except in the case of brief quotations embodied in critical articles and reviews.

For information address:

Scarlet Leaf Publishing House:

scarletleafpublishinghouse@gmail.com

DEDICATION

I dedicate this book to all the readers and all those who have encouraged me in my poetry-writing.

Vatsala Radhakeesoon   *   *Depth of the River*

Table of Contents

Acknowledgement I'm grateful to God for sustaining my inspiration and giving me the strength to write daily. 10

Author's Note 11

Life 13

    Antonyms in Life 14

    Detachment 15

    Embracing Freedom 16

    Grey, Blue 17

    Oh, Destiny 18

    Reflection Upon Life 19

    Simply an Observer 21

    Soulmates 22

    The Waterfall 23

    Depression and Reason 24

    Romantic Love vs God's Love 26

    My Little Daughter 29

    Egocentric Mirror of Illusion 31

    Prisoner of Desire 32

    Soul to Soul Love 33

    Living Confidently with Vitiligo 34

    Therapeutic Love 36

    True Love, at Last 38

Being Myself	39
Letting Go	40
What are We Rushing for?	42
From a Woman's Heart	44
The Light Within	46
Be the Gentlemen	47
Bangles	49
From an Intellectual Lady	52
Sweet Valentine's Day	54
Battle of Emotions	56
My Requests and My Dreams	60
Standing Alone	62
Connection	63
Moon and Night	64
Unite!	65
At the Café	67
Mystic Blue Sea	69
Music of Dawn	71
Little Lorenzo	73
The River's Poetess	75
Love	77
The Unique Velvet Leaf	80
Glimpses of Childhood	82
Separate Ways	86

- Being Positive 88
- Powerful Moon 89
- Standing against Violence 91
- Lover from Distant Seas 93

God/Spiritual Path 95
- A Yogi, A Brahmachari 96
- Connecting to Offwhite Light 98
- Death and After 99
- Spiritual Quest 100
- The Hermit Poet 101
- You and I 104
- Unique Connection 106
- Hymn to Brahma 108
- The Name of God 111

Biography –Vatsala Radhakeesoon 113

Afterword 115

Also By Vatsala Radhakeesoon 117

Acknowledgement

I'm grateful to God for sustaining my inspiration and giving me the strength to write daily.

I also thank my sister, Sharda, my brothers, Umesh and Comal, and my poet friend, Anoucheka Gangabissoon for their continual support while I've been writing this book

Author's Note

Life is like a river. It flows and we cannot stop it. The stages of life, that is, childhood, adolescence, adulthood and old age naturally flow. No human with a normal life span can skip any of those parts.

As far as there is life, happiness and sorrows will always keep on flowing. And it is only by going at the depth of this river-like life that we can see, understand and accept our lives as they truly are.

This book is divided into two parts: Life and God/Spirituality. Some of the poems in the first section are based on my personal experiences and they have been expressed as open confessions, and can be considered as the manifestation of my sub conscience. Other poems bring the social and global issues touching the lives of the whole human race and these poems have been written as philosophical reflections. The second part of this poetry book bring forth poems about the power of the creator of the universe and the maker of our lives, that is God. Much emphasis has also been laid on the undeniable fact that in this hectic mundane life, real peace, solace and joy can only be achieved by remaining connected to the Divine.

Poetry is also like a river. It is the flow of communication from the poet's pen to the hearts and souls of the readers. It invites the readers to first swim at the surface and then dive deep down to explore new horizons, new perceptions and new thoughts. Thus, the river-like Poetry can transform individual human beings as well as a whole society by broadening their knowledge and awareness. This in turn can lead to positive change, innovation and continuous progress in the world.

May the Divine Light enlighten the soul of each human being!

May each creature on Earth be blessed with love, peace and joy!

Vatsala Radhakeesoon

April 2017

Life

Antonyms in Life

Good, bad
Happy, sad
Kind, mean
Humble, arrogant
Cruel, forgiving
Selfless, selfish

Respect, disrespect
Truth, lies
Honesty, dishonesty
Sincerity, betrayal
Frankness, hypocrisy
Friendship, foehood

prevail in
Life's
actions
speech
mind

painting hearts
sunny blue
rainy grey

making us
wise
making us
blind.

Detachment

I still talk to all,
I still listen to all,
I still sympathize with all,
But now I'm detached from every soul

Embracing Freedom

Unsure love,
Painful shackles,
Repressed dreams,
Slave to ongoing trends
All-Mundane, all- fickle
To all these barriers
I say "No more."

Blue sky,
Warm sun,
Green island,
Perfect creation by the Divine;
Now I truly feel them,
Now I can really breathe,
Now I can genuinely live,
Now I am completely free.

Grey, Blue

Grey, Blue is my friend;
Like a wise man
he gives me philosophical advice.

In his vast lap,
 like a lover I rest my head;
The inner water and air he governs,
In soothing softness my darkness sails,
To a mind full of letters,
peace he always gives.

Oh, Destiny

Oh, Destiny!
Are you the clown's face, all-funny?
Are you the salty seawater, all- irony?
Are you the bright tropical sun, all-happy?
Are you the cyclonic night's rain, all- teary?

Oh, Destiny!
Are you my artful creator or
Am I your cautious maker?
I bet we are equal opportunity partners
in a game called Keep Life Rolling Better.

Oh, Destiny!
My colourless shadow,
Over the hills, my lingering echo,
Wherever I go, my breath you follow
Wherever you go, your hypnotic breeze I follow.

Reflection Upon Life

God has gifted me this life*
based on good and bad karmas of past life,
This hint from the sages I can't deny,
So I carry my basket of joys and sorrows
with a determined smile.

Pain and Pleasure-
What are they?
Do they really differ?
Are they somehow similar?

In silence, when I meditate
I often realize
Happiness and sadness are the results*
of present and previous life*,
They are the products of the same
unstable mind, all-unwise,
Holding on the former,
we fly in the sky of euphoria,
Engulfed by the latter,
we plunge in the sea of melancholia.

So, now I know that the best way to live freely
is like that of the cool and wise yogi
who has imbibed in his soul the true knowledge
that laughter and tears are just clouds of passing
fancies.

Author's Note:

Line 1: According to Vaidik dharma, when we are reborn we are born in a particular family, country and city according to our karmas performed in past life. Here, life refers to these basic issues.

Line 12 -13: According to Vaidik dharma, the results of the karmas lead to either happiness or sadness that we feel. These results of the karmas are obtained according to our good and bad deeds performed in both this life and previous life.

Simply an Observer

I stand on the bank
of the River of Experience,
I watch my own life
flowing by.

In my heart dwells
no laughter, no sigh;
Now, I'm simply an observer
of my thoughts, my emotions;
My mind can no longer cling on to
the futile mundane cadence.

Soulmates

No mundane taboos,
No hypocritical restrictions,
No fake rules

Simply drawn by the circle of light
so bright, so pure –
the energy of love
that has existed for eons,
and has been blessed by the Divine

Within it we have existed, co-existed,
We have lived, grown,
Within it we still exist, live,
We survive, shelter each other,
Within it we feel consumed, liberated,
We embrace mutual bliss, peace

Within this magnetic force, so soothing
dwell our subconscious minds, our souls
in eternal equilibrium, ongoing oneness.

The Waterfall

O continuously flowing waterfall!
Once again, at dawn,
you've called all the souls,
Some, liberated, invisible*
Others ,body-trapped, visible
At your command we are all servile
We are face to face with you,
Our hearts confessing without disguise

A soft, light pink feather has touched my chin
O sweet, generous, therapeutic waterfall!
Now I know what you mean
You want me to write poems on
nearby leaves quite thin
You want me to carve words of love on
each tropical flat stone amidst the green

O joyful, wise, soothing waterfall!
To your request
I acquiesce
Now, with permanent golden ink I write
so that all souls may read about hopeful love,
all-bright.

Author's Note:
liberated, invisible: According to Hinduism, after moksha (liberation of the cycle of birth and death), the soul can travel or visit any place as per its wish but normally it cannot interact with human beings.

Depression and Reason

In my 20's ,I have played
an impulsive game many times,
"Whether I slash my wrists
or jump off a cliff,
Who will care
where my soul treads?"
Thus spoke my heart
full of unfulfilled passion
lost in the rain
of hypnotic depression

"But isn't life larger than that?
Why don't I simply smile
and lie on the tropical beach
and shelter my thoughts
under God's luminous hat?"
Thus whispered the logic
of a saviour
carrying in his palm
the star of reason

"Depression, Reason,
Die, survive"
Those words swirled, churned
in the insomniac's dread /(fright)

"Enough!"

Vatsala Radhakeesoon * *Depth of the River*

said my spinning head
"Depression!
I kick you off",
"Reason!
In your lap I'll rest"

Up till my last breath
on a pink cloud,
I'll travel,
choosing the blue
and discarding the grey;
Like a warrior, I'll fight
for the gift called Life.

Romantic Love vs God's Love

In my 20's
I walked with a heart blurred and heavy,
wearing an alloyed chain of youth's dependency,
waiting for the love of the sun
and passion of the moon
to hug me tightly
and filled my life with permanent gaiety .

Now I'm thirty-nine,
No longer like a semi-open rose
But fully mature
and determined to listen to the
depth of my soul's voice

What a fool was I !
How ignorant was I!
These- I have now realized;
Mundane romantic love
is full of insecure, and futile sighs.

Many men try to impose their love on me,
They tell me that in old age
I'll have no one who will care for me
and I will feel all damn lonely,
I've learnt to listen to them un-reactively

and walk away bearing my feminine dignity.

To those who consider themselves
sheltered by a partner's love and lucky,
I bow to each of them and say sincerely
"May God bless thee!"

But to me true love
is the love of the Divine
and that's the type of love
that has touched my life.

When I close my eyes,
I deeply feel his rays
of love shining with
confidence amidst
his omniscience
his omnipresence
his omnipotence.

God loves me unconditionally,
And I too love him genuinely,
Unlike human heart,
his heart has no limited handcuffs,
It's all- space and eternal growth.

God's love always speaks the truth,
It's no flatterer,

but the wisest advisor
It shows me the enlightened path.

Being connected to God constantly,
I never feel lonely and unhappy ,
My life immerses in his immortality
And dances with his love's permanency.

My Little Daughter

O my little daughter!
Over the years,
you have smiled,
sung and played
in my imagination's garden,
But due to unpredictable circumstances
and my chosen life's broader mission
you have never been the fruition
of my reality's creation

Single and celibate ,
I've chosen to be
to protect you
from a fake daddy's
lies and treachery,
and the sharp tongue
of society's and family's mockery

O, my little daughter!
Amidst morning's poetry,
you have often hugged me
but now you have understood
that God and Poetry make me cheery,
So you have loosen your embrace
and set me free

You say that you are contented
in the unborn world,
Over there, no pain, no tears swirl
You are closer to the Divine,
At any time you can visit
any part of the universe
You are a liberated, unchained soul

O my little daughter!
My human soul feel a glimpse
of the distant future,
After many eons, you will again come
to me
As a mother, on Earth I will always be
your lighthouse
whenever you will sail in the vast sea
called life.

Egocentric Mirror of Illusion

O egocentric mirror of Illusion!
Reflections of illogical temptation,
Now, I recognize your claws of confusion

You paint the bad in glossy red
And the good in dull grey ,
You picture immorality as independence
And self-control as ignorance,
You smile at the selfish devil
And swear at the selfless angel

In your world, Darkness is the winner
And Light's brightness, the eternal loser

O egocentric mirror of illusion!
Yours is the upside-down
world of perfect chaos and degradation,
Now, I'm no longer blinded
by your hypocritical imagination,
My mind and soul flow in the stream
of pure and true divine revelation.

Prisoner of Desire

O Mind, selfish, lusty impulsive!
Now, you're burning in the flames
of Craving's fire,
Madly, you shout
"Life is meant solely for sensual pleasure"

You are like the colossal monster's mouth
wishing to gulp more and more,
You are the endless secret caves
dreaming to store your belonging more and more

O Mind, completely unbalanced, totally blind!
You can't perceive the truth that lies beyond,
You can't fathom the spiritual plane and rise
beyond

Your thoughts run with all pride
but even when your wishes are fulfilled,
You toss and turn amidst vulnerable nights
 grumbling "unsatisfied"

O Mind entrapped, unkind, unwise!
You're not a friend but your own foe,
Lust has made you a slave,
You are the prisoner of Desire.

Soul to Soul Love

Softly, silently, serenely you have touched my soul,
Our pangs locked in the prism of Sub conscience's past
now, though oneness, in unison seek liberation
And love with its lofty softness selflessly caresses, comforts, heals
our bruised, broken, bleeding hearts

Hand in hand, within the expanding, endless vastness
of pure, permanent white light we shine, smile
and peacefully fly beyond the monotonous mundane
to embrace the mystic, majestic flame of
the eternal energy of unconditional, unwavering true love

Past, present and future merge,
Eyes of the seer, eyes of omnipresent God –
they can see our lives, our undying love
and daily they bless our miraculous mission:
First to heal ourselves through the power of love
and in turn through boundless compassion
to soothe the pain of the entire planet Earth.

Living Confidently with Vitiligo

When I was ten,
white depigmented patches hit
my tropically tanned skin,
Doctors diagnosed it as Vitiligo –
A disorder whose causes and treatments
were still obscure
but it was the ongoing subject
of medical research for sure

Though I was prescribed medicines
that could safeguard the remaining melanin
and my condition didn't harm anybody else
the society gripped my surroundings
in its claws cruelly,
Many thought my condition to be ugly and scary,
Others called my life a disgrace to feminine
beauty
They deliberately at all cost shunned my
company

But determined was I not to bow
at the ignorant arrows of injustice,
I kept on walking fearlessly
amidst the serene greenery,
I looked up at the blue sky
and could feel God hugging me securely,
I listened to the musicality of the waves
and as they touched my bare feet they whispered
" True beauty lies in the immortal soul,
   Physical beauty tarnishes,

It never embraces eternity."

Thus, for years, Nature has remained
my true companion,
Its divine solitude
has taught me to be emotionally independent,
It has taught me
to be myself,
It has given me my own voice –
my voice flowing in Poetry

I have discovered my true self,
I have learnt to live,
live freely, with no psychological blocks or complexes
live wisely by being immune to the negative mentality
live confidently with my disorder –
the non-segmental Vitiligo.

Therapeutic Love

My heart, once
bruised
broken
shattered
now daily feels
the halo-like light
of soft love

The warmth of
your muscular, masculine arms
knocks down
my self-built fortress
of alienation,
my illusive cocoon
of mental blocks

Your kisses
deep,
passionate
now reassures me
that I can love again

And as we melt
in each other
smiles at us
perfect union,
perfect creation,

Vatsala Radhakeesoon * *Depth of the River*

the expansion
of multi-dimensional creativity
leading to
our fruitful, healthy growth
as two writers.

True Love, at Last

Like an elegant knight
he softly holds my hand,
Lovingly, he imprints
protective kisses on my forehead

In contrast to my past-
Scars and bruises
left by mechanical love,
all this is so different

I touch the tropical greenness,
O my God! This is real,
On his chest my head rests
In his strong arms deep love swirls

Sometimes I'm lost again in oblivion –
in some tinges of worries, all-grey
but his ardent kisses chase away
my mood swings, my illusion –
my insecure imagination

As we hold each other tight
we can see through our souls' eyes
all the Gods in heaven smiling
and showering us with their divine blessings.

Being Myself

I walk hand in hand with
justice
peace
tolerance

I reject all forms of
degradation
discrimination
humiliation

Since I take life too seriously
I'm often alienated by
the shallow,
vainly laughing
mocking crowd

But now I've learnt
not to despair
not to cry

By being connected to
my creator – the Divine
and letting the light
within my soul brightly shine
I keep on walking alone
towards my destined path – my mission
with a victorious smile.

Letting Go

Lost Love
Shattered dreams
Careless thoughts
Reckless actions
Tactless speeches
of yesterday, the past –
Daily, gradually
I'm learning
to cling to them
no more

Now, I take
a deep breath,
I release them
from my mind,
I spread wide
the wings of wisdom,

I fly to
the light
within my soul,
There I discover
the golden keys –
 All-authentic
All-original
All-selfless
All- egoless,

These are how

the Creator wants
human beings
to really be,
These are what
will open the doors to
Real Freedom,
True Life,
Eternal bliss.

What are We Rushing for?

What are we rushing for?
Blind wealth?
Arrogant fame?
Superficial love?

We have been taught
to reach the goals very fast
to be always the Number 1
in the rat race
Even relationships need to be
planned, systematic, down to Earth

In pursuit of this illusory mundane,
We often become
stressed, depressed,
antipathic, egoistic,
inhumane, vain

O Human Race!
O Friends!
What are we rushing for?

It is shallow
nothingness,
nullity
dullness
It is a living death

Let's take a deep breath,
Learn to let everything go,

Vatsala Radhakeesoon * *Depth of the River*

No bonds, no pain, no regrets
Let's connect to
the divine
the soul within us

Over there we always find
Peace,
Liberation,
Bliss

O Human Race!
O Friends!
The essence of human life is
to discover the true self
to know the real God

Life often calls for a halt in
sublime silence,
perfect peace
It wishes our minds, bodies and souls
be merged in the wise poise

So, Human Race,
My dear friends,
What are we rushing for?

From a Woman's Heart

I am a woman
created by God
with much tenderness,
Blessed am I
with the rights
to love a gentleman
who knows how to treat ladies
with unfailing fairness

For my true love
I want to
dress up always elegantly,
smile sometimes shyly,
coin words at times wittily,
laugh often intelligently

When I see sadness
flickering in his eyes,
I let my feminine honesty
pacify his silent cries

I often hold his hand softly
assuring him that his painful battle
will never be lonely,
For eons, by his side
he'll always have God and me

When I see happiness
sparkling in his eyes,

Vatsala Radhakeesoon * *Depth of the River*

I let my love swim
to his divine smiles

He holds me tightly
and I let my soft kisses
tell him confidently
how much I'm proud of
his daily caring gestures,
his risky heroic tasks,
everything that he does for me

For my true love,
I pray that light fills his life,
I pray for his good health
and longevity

All our dreams, our sacrifices
will merge
and together for several lives
we'll live blissfully
in our expanding, growing
circle of pure love.

The Light Within

Whether you cut me
with blade-like words,
Whether your male chauvinism
mocks my feminine dreams,
The light within me – the soul
will eternally be alive

I may bend, bleed
by your violent, manly blows
Your wickedness may smile
like a winner
but my Creator – the Divine
will always lift
the light within me
and again *la tête haute*
I will walk like
the Egyptian queen

O, Cruel Man!
A disgrace to all gentlemen,
A shame to manhood,
Open your eyes,
Rise beyond your fake power,
Rest assured that your injustice
can never extinguish
the un-flickering light within
all women.

Be the Gentlemen

Slim or athletic
but always
the physically stronger ones,
O, Men!
God has created you
with all his mightiness

You've been blessed with
brave knightly chests,
wise practical minds,
speeches and actions
of the Leaders

But O, Men –
God's beloved children!
Over the years,
what have many men become?

Men who are lost
in the dark,
Please , open your eyes,
Rise beyond your fake
anger,
ego,
superiority complex,
Connect to the true elements
of your creation

Along your Life's paths
You often come across

some good women –
God created children
carrying the softness
of petals-like bodies
but inner strength
of the blessed life-givers

They are not your prey
but respectable helpers,
They are not your foes
but supportive friends,
Respect them,
They will respect you,
Value their hearts, minds
and souls,
They will value yours,
Hold their hands
with dignity,
They will always
be there for you

So Men,
Be your true selves!
Claim your real rights!
You are not meant to be
destructively domineering,
You are meant to be
the confident, selfless gentlemen.

Bangles

Bangles are beautiful,
Some are colourful,
Some are golden,
Some are silvery,
some are gold-plated

When I was a child,
Mum insisted that I wore
the valuable shiny ones
on special occasions,
and the delicate metallic ones
on a daily basis

But growing up
with two brothers,
I always joined in
I enjoyed
 the climbing on trees
the pirate games,
So, amidst my rushing, running,
jumping, ambush-hiding,
my bangles always lost
their original shapes,
and on my wrists,
the distorted ovalness rebelled

Mum felt embarrassed
as I was her careless,
clumsy daughter

but never was I vexed
to be unlike the stylish girls

When I was a teenager,
Rules forbade
the wearing of bangles
at schools,
"What a relief " I thought,
Liberated was I from
the cumbersomeness

As an adult,
I've chosen
to remain single,
Never have I been
the Asian bride,
the Asian wife
compelled to wear
the bangles
believed to be
the emblem of
family prosperity

However, gradually
I've learnt to appreciate
the bangles
and when I attend
some grand festivity
or cultural ceremony,
I, at times wear
the bangles
as my choice

Vatsala Radhakeesoon * *Depth of the River*

but never
as an ornament
of obligation

Now, my wrists
have learnt
to carry them
with feminine grace.

From an Intellectual Lady

Like most women,
I'm also interested
in beauty care and dresses
but mine is a classic, practical style:
Some short hair
that can easily be smoothed
and look perfectly neat,
Some sober lipstick
that matches my thoughtful speeches,
Some expressive eye make-up
that blends with my pensive look,
some elegant casual and formal wear
that reflect logic and orderliness

However, dressing and eating habits
are for me the trivialities
of daily routine,
Never do they stand out
among my topics of conversations

My main subjects of interests are
Books – classics , contemporaries,
Books of Arts, Science, Philosophy,
History, Politics, Spirituality
and any other field
that enhance knowledge

I read books

with an analytical mind,
I have my views,
my appreciation,
my constructive criticism
Never am I scared
to say them aloud,
to write them boldly on paper

I have a humane heart,
I can talk to anyone tactfully,
I can sympathize with them genuinely
but my close friends are
those who value profundity
and reject all forms of mediocrity

I live for
cultivating and awakening the mind
as well as encouraging others to do so,
I live for
the progress of the entire Human Race.

Sweet Valentine's Day

From Love's womb, we've been born,
Its heart is our true abode,
Wisely for centuries
it has sustained human sub conscience

In poems
In paintings,
In songs
or other forms of Arts,
Love has always been
the pillar,
the backbone,
the undying echo

Today is Love's Day – Valentine's Day,
Red roses
Satin hearts
Soft teddy bears
Chocolate boxes
Candlelit dinners
Sweet memories
smile elegantly in the air

It's a unique day
to make promises of eternal love,
to propose the beloved,
to kiss and cuddle passionately

O, Human Race!
On this sweet Valentine's Day,

Vatsala Radhakeesoon *　　*Depth of the River*

Let's flow with the rhythm of love,
Let's join in
Let's celebrate!

Battle of Emotions

In an elliptic
bubble-like transparent
but waterproof, shockproof
rotating laboratory,
amidst the volcanic regions
of Planet Numb
echoed the laughter
of Green Fangs –
the Ruler, the King

Half dragon-like,
Half centaur-like,
Such a creature
was unknown to Earth

Grinned Green Fangs
at the frowning test-tubes
on the golden racks

"Planet Earth, I'm landing,
Emotions Exterminate!"
he roared

In a fluffy
soft cotton wool-like
candy floss pink
serene castle
amidst the sunny lands
of Golden Beach Island

Vatsala Radhakeesoon   *   *Depth of the River*

vibrated the aura
of Rainbow Light –
the saviour, the guardian

A genteel unicorn
with an illuminated
ruby ornament on its forehead,
A true friend,
A genuine master,
The apple of the eye
of Earth's inhabitants

Through the meditative third eye
Rainbow Light captured
rays of the venomous mission,
As dark fumes,
it spat it ,
it rejected it

" Planet Earth, I'll protect you,
Emotions remain still!"
it exclaimed

Green Fangs kept on injecting
on Planet Earth
his new inventions –
the powerful vaccines:
Anti-compassion,
Anti-care,
Anti-love,
Anti bravery,
Anti-fear,

Anti-joy,
Anti- sorrows,
Anti - all emotions

Rainbow Light on each
terrestrial corner
spread its defence mechanisms –
the reliable potions:
100% Empathy,
100% care,
100% love,
100% bravery,
100% happiness,
100% grief,
100% all-emotions balanced

The overly tensed battle
went on for hours,
At last, Rainbow Light
with its unfailing
positive thoughts' shield
hit Green Fangs' master-mind,
It disintegrated into
a silvery magnetic rod,
Then it evaporated as fumes
black, navy-blue, grey,
all blended.

Leapt with joy
on the rotating Earth
Rainbow Light –

the protective unicorn,
Mother Earth hugged him,
kissed him,

All emotions on Planet Earth
merrily danced like Bacchus's followers,
The were safe,
They were free.

My Requests and My Dreams

When I was a child,
you often gifted me dolls,
Now, that I'm a teenager,
you often buy me
the latest bangles,
the shiny earrings,
the fashionable dresses,
You instil in me motherhood and
wifehood at even a very young age

Maa, I don't deny
my feminine functions,
but please, Maa,
no longer gift me
superficial ornaments
for my birthdays,
I'm comfortable in
my practical tops
and blue jeans

Maa, please buy me
books – Classics , contemporaries,
books of Literature, Science,
books of History, Psychology.
books of Spirituality, Philosophy

All I wish is to
broaden my knowledge,
develop a logical, analytical mind,

Vatsala Radhakeesoon   *   *Depth of the River*

speak aloud my views fearlessly

All that I wish is to be
a cultivated, intellectual woman,
a profound woman of true dignity.

Standing Alone

Truth, Justice, Honesty –
These paths are often lonely
but to my heart, mind and soul,
they are perfectly friendly

Shallowness, Cowardice, Hypocrisy, Mediocrity
sing the comfort zone song –
the mundane song
amidst the huge crowd
but I refuse to join in

I'm often called "Stupid"
I'm often called "Naive"
I'm often called "Loser"
But I don't give in

I'm not scared to walk alone,
I'm not solitude phobic,
For some fake, temporary happiness
never will I sell my soul

Up till my last breath,
I will stand alone if I have to
because I know that
within me there's a leader, a winner
Someone, somewhere on Earth
always has to bell the cat.

Connection

O cute kitten!
Your manila envelope-coloured coat
is velvet soft, unique,
As your innocent blue eyes meet mine
and your small paws rest on my hand,
instantly I can feel the intensity
of some light divine

You and I –
both parts of Creation,
Cut from the same unifying thread,
Sculpted, moulded
by the same artist, immortal hand
surely, we have some deep connection

O cute kitten!
My soul does feel, knows
that you and I
have distinct roles, functions
but yet we are meant to live
in perfect harmony on Planet Earth
and sing the song of equilibrium

O Cute kitten!
I promise you
never will I hurt you,
never will I ignore you,
I will always protect you.

Moon and Night

*(based on the painting Dance at Dawn
by Irish artist Linda Ibbotson)*

Knightly Moon peeps through the trees
at Night, his beauty queen;
So calm, soothing and refreshing she looks
as her enchanting dark robe
gradually embraces Aurora's first ray

Before she's fully awake,
Moon , the ardent lover
implants a kiss on her *or rosé* lips

Then, softly he whispers
"Darling Night, now I must take leave,
I let you wear your dutiful dress
all-sparkling with light ,
Please obey the orders of the Creator;
Again in the darkness we shall meet,
All-carefree we shall rest in each other's arms;
O, Night, my sweetheart!
You will always be mine."

Unite!

With the same love intensity,
With the hands of equality,
the perfect one – the Divine
has created all human beings,
all other creatures

Each soul though unique
is made up of
the same basic components,
the same light

So, Human Race,
in the name of religion,
in the name of race,
in the name of skin colour,
let's fight no more

Extinguish the flames of
nonsensical ego,
illogical hatred,
false pride,
fake self-images

O, Human Race!
Unite! Unite!
Let's be one –
one global family
that holds hands, smiles;
Let's be the biggest star

that shines brightly,
and safeguards planet Earth peacefully.

At the Café

Half absent-mindedly,
he entered the café;
He took a seat,
His hair was somewhat dishevelled,
His eyes were puffy,
He forced a grin
as he ordered Espresso coffee,
Though he looked like a creature
of sleepless nights,
Apollonian beauty traced his face

"Who was he?" I wondered
Hooked by him was my inspiration

Some inner force gathered within me,
I sat beside him,
His defensive eyes shot the lines
"Miss...I need my solitude, my space",
"So do I" answered my confident smile

"But what if he was waiting
for his date or his wife?"
Questions swirled in my mind
for a while

Some comments about the weather,
Some observations about the unusual music,
A glimpse at a long working day,
All these were enough to break the ice

Vatsala Radhakeesoon * *Depth of the River*

Harsh reality spoke,
Scars of past divorce
tainted his thoughts,
Bruises of the unmarried heart
unlocked from my sub conscience

The two extremes, of course we were
but the realization of the futility of
uncertain bondage, chained emotions
shined as intersection points

Our laughter were
at times cynical,
at times wrapped in
Je m'en foutisme,
Yet at the depth of our hearts
still beat the desire
to love without ego, without expectations,
to love with maturity, with wisdom,
to love freely

Mesmerized by each other,
we promised to be friends;
"I will write your story" I said
He grinned,
In his eyes instantly beamed
Hope – A new beginning.

Mystic Blue Sea

O, mystic blue sea
of my rainbow island,
tropical island, so exotic!

In you I confide these:

Tonight with a white A4 sheet
I've created a paper boat,
With some red ink,
I've practised some calligraphy,
On both sides,
the word 'Moonbeams'
could be read

Then in the paper boat,
I've enclosed
a love poem written
on some light paper, all-pink
and a well- chiselled velvet heart
that sings the love of my heartbeats

O mystic blue sea!
Now, in your lap,
I entrust my white boat,
Protect it against
the luring mermaid's songs
and the strong winds,
Carry my love
to my lover
who is struggling

on distant shores

O, mystic blue sea!
At sunset, I can now hear
your waves reciting my lines
"Dear lover ,
your mesmerizing beauty
has sealed my heart,
I can see you, feel you
everywhere;
For eons, I'm ready
to wait for you,
and remain faithful
to our undying
soul to soul love."

Music of Dawn

I see big, small, minute circles
as I close my eyes,
Circles and circles are everywhere,
swirls, swirls my soul around them,
They play the music of dawn –
Silence

Silence isn't sound-less,
It can be heard solely
with the ears of the soul
detached from the mundane,
unbound by the illusive permanence

The music of dawn
comes from the notes of the harp
played by the Divine,
It calms the mind
by injecting positive thoughts,
It pacifies the heart
by discarding the broken parts,
It enlightens the soul
by drawing us closer
to the light supreme

I plunge, plunge
in the music of dawn,
I feel free, liberated
from the mask imposed,
I feel relieved, unburdened
from the constraints, all-vain

Vatsala Radhakeesoon   *   *Depth of the River*

To the music of dawn
dances the genuine, true self –
The self that is not limited
by the common "Me" and "I",
The self that expands, grows,
unifies with a whole,
The self that becomes
blissful music itself,
The self that dwells permanently
as inner peace within
the entire creation,
The self that is the seed
of universal love.

Little Lorenzo

He came in my life
as a cute baby –
My little Lorenzo
with big brown eyes

Now he's three
but different from others,
When I call his name
he still doesn't respond,
He's scared of visitors
and avoids eye contact at all cost,
His words, his sentences
are incoherent, incomplete, repetitive;
He flaps his hands
and asks for a frog toy obsessively

For a while, his behaviour
worried me, confused me
but by now I know he's autistic –
My only special child

He is now on ongoing therapy;
I've learnt to
appreciate his unique ways,
celebrate his own successes,
observe non-verbal clues,
play with him,
protect him

Vatsala Radhakeesoon   *   *Depth of the River*

As he grins,
my maternal heart melts,
I hug him tight, kiss his forehead
and whisper in his ears,
" My son, I will always love you."

Vatsala Radhakeesoon   *   *Depth of the River*

The River's Poetess

By the River of Happiness,
I often meet a poetess,
She has been blessed with
beauty like that of a goddess,
Her smile is as innocent as a child
shinning in dawn's freshness

Sometimes she jumps
from rock to rock,
At times she rests
her right ear
on the flowing water

"What are you doing?"
I can't help asking her

"I'm a child of Nature"
she usually says,
With a divine pen
gifted to me by Athena,
I daily write poems
on water,
Then the powerful winds
carry them at
the depth of the river;

You have to let your ear
caress the water all-clear,
and listen, listen with

both mundane eyes closed
but opening the inner eyes
like those of greatest seers;
You will hear, all the time hear
my poems beings read aloud
by mystical water-nymphs
in a voice somewhat musical,
in a voice from the land of No Fear"

Mesmerized am I
by this river's poetess,
Now, for many years
I have known her,
She understands my aims
and fears,

We have become
the best of friends –
Moi – the poetess
surrounded by endless
worries, desires and ambitions
of fast-moving urban life,
and *Elle* – the poetess
all free , carefree and stress-free
constantly connected to blissful
tropical greenness of rural life.

Love

O, Love!
First, you showed me
your fangs,
Lies,
Betrayal,
Misunderstanding,
Scorn,
Shallowness

Clouds of Sufferings
poured in my heart,
My mind danced
under illusory tunes,
Thoughts and judgments
cried under the tree
of misbalance ,

O, Love!
In my life,
for years
you stood as
unpractical Madness.

O, Love!
But now ,
what are all these?
You show me
the sun of wisdom,
the blue sky of

mystical eternal love,
the warm hugs of
roses, sunflowers
and humble trees

The rainbow of peace
sings in my heartbeats,
My mind is itself
a joyful garden of solace,
Thoughts and perceptions
no longer master me

O, Love!
In my life,
you currently
showers bliss.

But Love,
What is your true nature?
What is your real-self?
I've been pondering
and pondering for months,

And by now, I know
you are like two-faced Janus –
Part of you smile ,
Another part sighs

O, Love!
Today I've nothing
to reproach you,
You have taught me

Vatsala Radhakeesoon   *   *Depth of the River*

lessons of pains,
lessons of joy,
You have taught me
to live,
All that I can say is
"Thank you Love!"

The Unique Velvet Leaf

I breathe the tropical breeze,
A large *feuille velours* – velvet leaf
has just flown to me,
Now it rests on my wrist
like a big watch

A poem in natural violet
elegantly smiles on it,
The unique velvet leaf itself
from time to time read these lines:

" Dear Lady, Never fear!
Distance is just a mirage,
an ode to mere Illusion;
Closer and closer, each second
our hearts beat in unison,
Our souls for eons
have travelled on lands
and in space,
My sweetheart, our love
is the anchor, the governor
of smooth sailing life,
So my dear lady,
Be confident, be wise
 you're never alone,
Never so you will be

Vatsala Radhakeesoon   *   *Depth of the River*

This unique velvet leaf
from my handsome lover
is to me very dear,
I keep it as a bookmark
for my poetry books,
It makes me feel daily
that love and poetry
are my guardian angels
and in my life security
is always near

Glimpses of Childhood

When I close my eyes,
glimpses of childhood
at me smile,
I re-live the earlier years
of my urban life

Morning time:
The tropical sky was painted
in natural blue,
The hot sun shone
magnanimously above Corps De Garde
mountain – the armour, the protector
of Rose-Hill Town.

I was only three,
too young to go
to primary school then,
Mother preferred I stayed
at home with *Nani** on that day
My two brothers – 5 and 6 years
older than me respectively
were ready to go to school,
My parents, both teachers
also left for work

All gone to tackle
their busy days,
I was left with Nani;

Vatsala Radhakeesoon   *   *Depth of the River*

For me she safely kept
the lemon, orange, coffee candies
and chocolate flavoured Maucob toffees

I took five candies,
put them in my dress pocket
and rushed outside,
For me, a sunny day
meant simply fun and play

With no other child of
my age in the neighbourhood,
I was alone,
I devised my own games,
my own rules –
Running fast,
Rabbit Jump
Hiding behind trees,
Ambush to warrior cat,
All these maintained
my senses active, alert

Noon was lunch time,
Unlike other kids,
I wasn't food-fussy,
Those were the days
I ate without worry,
but my favourite was
the dessert undoubtedly

After lunch, I wasn't allowed
to play in the afternoon sun,

Vatsala Radhakeesoon   *   *Depth of the River*

I stayed inside (indoors),
amidst my soft toys, dolls
and cubic puzzles

Once I asked Nani
to make a dress for Teddy,
Her hands moving
on the sewing machine
reflected her magical mastery

Within 3 hours,
a pink flowery frock
was at me waving,

Teddy wore it elegantly,
Proud was I that she looked
like a decent girl,
"She is my transformed Little friend"
I thought

At 3.30 pm, when my parents
came back home,
I always assured them
that I'd been a good girl,
No single mischief was ever done;
They smiled but their eyes
like those of most parents,
especially like those of most teachers
frankly said
" Yes we know,
   These are white lies".

Vatsala Radhakeesoon   *   ***Depth of the River***

***Nani**: (from Hindi) maternal grandmother*

Separate Ways

We dreamt of a home
amidst the greenery,
We dreamt of a
united family

At first, we could live
with our differences,
but soon Intolerance
banged its fists

He was a party animal,
He stayed late at nights
to places unknown to me,
but I knew he enjoyed
one night stands with
the painted faced girls

I wished to love
only one man,
but my nights were spent
waltzing with words
on my laptop screen

One early morning,
we could no longer
stand each other,
Each comment, each view
turned out into a dispute

Vatsala Radhakeesoon   *   *Depth of the River*

Coldly we said goodbye,
our hearts singing
the song of relief,

We went our separate ways,
and never ever
did our eyes meet again.

Being Positive

Every day we smile
to hide the bitter bruises
of the past,
We paint a rainbow
in the void
of the present,
We hope for
the wisdom of sunshine
in the future

And the song of Subconscious
– the inner voice that sustains us
keeps singing constantly this chorus
"Go on, go on, my friend;
Fight, fight for Positivity
 up till the life-battle ends.

Powerful Moon

Tonight the moon
is my page,
With the luminous ink
of the stars,
I write lines of verses
for the human race

O, Humanity!
Wake up!,
Breathe, Feel
the coolness
of the moon rays!

As they will penetrate
your mind, body and soul,
All knots of anguish
will disentangle,
All fangs of hatred
will detoxify,
and The flower of love
on Planet Earth will smile

O, Human Race –
My dear friends!
Tonight as messenger
of the moon,
I've delivered to you
that message,
I pray that you live
a life of wisdom

Vatsala Radhakeesoon * *Depth of the River*

and unfailing grace.

Standing against Violence

The sky is grey,
The bombs and guns fill
in the air,
Nature's beauty is stained
by barbarous bloodshed,
Hopes, dreams and freedom
are smashed within seconds

Men, women and children –
Each of them have a heart,
Each of them have a soul,
Mental peace,
Protective love,
Blissful joy
are the birth rights of each

So, selfish, disillusioned killers,
Please don't snatch their rights,
their needs,
Please put an end to
the unjustified hatred,
the fruitless violence

My Poetic Voice
will keep on shouting ,
"Please stop,
Please stop,
Please stop,"

until you really stop.

Lover from Distant Seas

O, Lover from distant seas!
It's only for you that
my heart strongly beats

Though I've met you
only a few times,
I feel we've known
each other for eternity
in the cycle of endless lives

When you can't answer
my phone calls,
You can't reply to
my e-mails and
Facebook messages,
logically I do understand
that you are busy, my love
but my emotional heart sinks
deep down in a pool
of invisible tears,
then floats on a grey cloud
of scary , gloomy anxiety

I wonder whether
you are eating properly,
I wonder whether
you can sleep at nights,
I wonder whether
you are really taking care

of your life

O, my love!
I wish so much
to wrap my arm around
your muscular thighs,
to rest my head
on your manly chest,
to listen to
your soothing heartbeats,

O, my love!
I really wish
to feel your long legs
securing my frail body,
to feel your passionate kisses
driving me to real ecstasy

O, my lover from distant seas!
I do worry about you,
I do miss you,
So, my love,
daily I pray
"Please come to me,
Take me home,
Let's unite
and forever be one."

God/Spiritual Path

Vatsala Radhakeesoon   *   *Depth of the River*

A Yogi, A Brahmachari

I met a *yogi*, a *brahmachari*,
Little did he speak to me,
But I felt in many lives,
he'd been guiding me.

The Yoga *aasans* –
he knew them all,
To seekers he taught them all,
He said,
"Yoga blesses good health to all".

The *Vedas*, The *Upnishads* –
he'd studied them all,
In his eyes sparkled knowledge
like bright gold,
His sermons spread   unveiled truth,
wisdom for all.

In his presence shone discipline bold,
In his charisma glowed faith in God,
From his smile wise to all zeal flowed.

yogi *(from Hindi and Sanskrit): A person who performs yoga, meditation and has reached a high spiritual level. He is detached from the materialistic world, leads a life of discipline and self-control.*

Brahmachari *(from Hindi and Sanskrit): An unmarried person who has chosen celibacy for a lifetime.*

aasans *(from Hindi): postures performed in yoga*

Vedas*: The main religious/sacred book of Hinduism*

Upnishads*: An important sacred book of Hinduism*

Connecting to Offwhite Light

I close the mundane blurred eyes,
Within seconds, open the inner eyes, all-bright,
Now I can see some light off white
It's neither linear, nor spherical
but homogeneous, continuous, undoubtedly
eternal.

To the off white light
that generates the universe generously
now connects the subtlest, the minutest part
within me.

I have no fears,
I feel no anger,
I don't have vain questions
to answer,
To the Divine I feel closer,
I dwell in a realm genuinely safer.

Death and After

Wait, wait, I'm coming!
Neither am I scared nor screaming,
With joy my eyes are dancing,
I can hear Divine Music echoing.

Feel, now, O, Detached Soul, you surely can!
Feel pure light, perfect knowledge of Immortal Friend;
Fly freely to all planets, you surely can!
It's All- blissful, no sorrows to mend.

Spiritual Quest

From land to land I did travel,
All I saw was Regret's well,
Some Acharyas, some seers I of course met,
But in the Fallen Era many have offset Spiritual Mindset.

My head rested on the greener wet grass,
Gazing the sky to Almighty God I asked
'Without Genuine Guru, how will I Spiritual Tests pass?'

God softly held my hand,
He said 'Nurse no fears my friend,
The Divine Knowledge I've safeguarded beforehand,
Read them when to your Inner Voice I command,
Connect deeply to me and the Truth you'll understand.'

God himself was the True Teacher I realized,
AUM., Omnipresent in Egoless Minds also resides,
Within us his powerful light he always casts,
reminding us to embrace Good Karmas till Life-breath lasts.

The Hermit Poet

I

'Let's go to the forest' whisper my feet,
A wise tree with cool leaves is my seat,
Colourful birds all-free wake up and greet
Aurora's beauty which no Human artistry can defeat.

In the lotus position, merrily I sit,
Distracting bonds in my mind like drums beat.

Rule 1 is: Never panic by Maya's* tricks,
Rule 2 is: Be aware of all hindrances shouting 'Weak',
Rule 3 is: Let go of all obstructions that to Mind-Wild sneak.

Rule 4 is: Gently, softly let the agitated mind tranquilize,
Rule 5 is: Zealously, happily go back to Mindfulness of Breathing all-wise.

To this hermit- life I'm new,
Obstacles are at times many, at times few;
But the Enlightened One* is my Guru,
His Dhamma* helps my life to grow, expand, renew.

Spiritual efforts and investigation I'll never quit,
The five precepts* are my Daily Principles' kits.

The Four Noble Truths*, The Suttas*-in them I plunge each day,
Meditation practice tests me, smiles at me in its peculiar ways.

Bonds, bonds-I've severed them all,
Supramundane Nibbana* is the ultimate goal,
'But to it never be attached too' advise the masters bold.

II

In blissful solitude, amidst lovely Nature
flow in verse my spiritual quest, my experiences on paper;
Thank you Enlightened One to be my muse, my caretaker.

To the world I give some poetry,
O Readers, rise beyond All-Mundane and be happy!

Maya: Illusion

Enlightened One: The Buddha

Dhamma: The teachings, the doctrine

Five Precepts: Referring to the 5 precepts of Buddhism:

1. I shall not kill
2. I shall not steal
3. I shall not be involved in sexual misconduct
4. I shall not lie
5. I shall not take toxic and harmful substances such as alcohol and drugs

The Four Noble Truths: This refers to the basic teachings of Buddhism:

1. *Suffering (Dukkha)*
2. *The arising/origin of suffering (Samudaya)*
3. *The cessation of suffering (Nirodha)*
4. *The way leading to the cessation of suffering (Magga)*

The Suttas: discourses /sermons of The Buddha

Nibbana: Ultimate Reality, Abslute Truth, Freedom from the cycle of birth and death

You and I

You and I
have known
each other
for eons

You know
my present,
my future
my past

You shelter
my frail body
with your light,
all-divine
You nurture
my immortal soul
with Knowledge,
all-true

You are
everywhere I go
O, omnipresent Power!
In your invisible eyes
you hold
my life

Sometimes
in sansara
I stumble, I swirl

Vatsala Radhakeesoon * *Depth of the River*

I jump, I juggle
amidst
the labyrinth, the loop
of tricky Sorrow

Then, you grip
my mind
and say
"Stand up,
  Be firm,
  Not blind"

O, good Lord!
O, compassionate God!
You and I
have a connection
perfect,
pure,
sincere,
unbreakable

O, God!
forever yours
I shall be.

Unique Connection

My connection with you is unique,
It's unlike the earthy bonds that are
illusive and weak.

When I want to meet you,
When I wish to talk to you,
I don't need to take   appointments, make calls
or in any other way be formal.

Whenever I wish to feel you deeply,
I close my eyes gently,
I shut the doors of thoughts all-worldly,
I connect to your divine light instantly.

O, God!
O, adorable Divine!
In your omniscience, omnipresence
my soul plunges,

I feel something growing,
something expanding,
I feel eternity,
I feel immortality.

O, God!
O, Creator of Kindness!
I'm sheltered
by your togetherness,

Vatsala Radhakeesoon * *Depth of the River*

your closeness
your oneness

When I connect with you daily
 nothing within me
remain stifled,
painfully crushed

You give me
more and more space,
My body, mind and soul harmonize
I'm like a light flying feather, absolutely free.

Hymn to Brahma

In dawn's solitude smiles
the serene,
newly-born,
carefree,
pure
atmosphere

My body,
soul,
mind
are deaf
to all hectic sounds,
All-mundane

All that I can hear
is this hymn-
A hymn to Brahma –
God,
The Creator,
The Divine

My sub conscience says
This divine song
has been there
for eternity

"O, Brahma!
O, Light,
O, Space

Vatsala Radhakeesoon   *   *Depth of the River*

Infinite!

O, Omniscient,
Omnipotent,
Omnipresent
Maker!

You are
All -Knowledge,
The Absolute,
Flawless

As I connect to you,
I know myself –
the immortal soul,
the perishable body,
I recognize you –
the Supreme Soul,
My creator,
The artist,
The architect
The birth-giver
of the universe

O, Brahma!
I know that
only from you,
I'll find

true peace,
real knowledge,
unfailing love

You are wholesome,
You'll make me
wholesome for aeons."

The Name of God

The Vedas say
"AUM is the main
 name of God,
He is omniscient,
He is omnipresent,
He is omnipotent"

When I talk and talk
for a whole day,
I feel tired, drained;
I just want to shut all
doors of reactive senses

But when I sit cross-legged,
close my eyes, breathe deeply
and chant His name
"AUM, AUM, AUM...
3 times, 108 times or even more,
all fatigue is gone,
I feel energized,
my soul expanding with
calmness and universal love,
I feel all-renewed,
ready to face the world as it is.

Vatsala Radhakeesoon   *   *Depth of the River*

Biography –Vatsala Radhakeesoon

Born in Mauritius in 1977, Vatsala Radhakeesoon has had a keen interest in poetry-writing since the age of 14. Her poems have been previously published in various local and international printed and online newspapers, journals, magazines, anthologies and blogs. She is the representative of Immagine and Poesia (Italy based artistic movement) for Mauritius.

Vatsala considers Poetry to be her first love, her friend, guide and confidant.

As a teenager in the early 1990's, her love for poetry mainly originated from the lyrics of songs of the French Canadian singer, Roch Voisine, Australian singer, Jason Donovan and British singer Phil Collins. Her mother being a Hindi teacher and her best teacher of poetry has also been her inspiration for poetry-writing. The great poets of English Literature, William Blake, T.S Eliot, Emily Dickinson, Maya Angelou and Carol Ann Duffy have had an influence on her works. Depth of the River is her second collection of poems following When Solitude Speaks (2013).

Vatsala Radhakeesoon is a MBA graduate from Management College of Southern Africa and is currently self-employed. She lives at Rose-Hill,

Mauritius and continues to write poems in English, Mauritian Kreol (Kreol Morisien), French and Hindi.

Afterword

Poetry is a form of creative writing that has much depth. Life, if taken philosophically, also expresses its very profundity on a daily basis.

Depth of the River is the author's second collection of poems emphasizing on her life as it is. She considers this book as her open confessions manifesting from her subconscious mind.

This book also brings forth, social and global issues that touch the Human race, as a whole. Through her poems, the poet has also pointed out that the connection to the Divine energy, that is God, is the best cure to all sufferings and the priceless means to recognizing real joy and leading a peaceful life.

The poems in this book have been written by blending elements of modern and traditional poetry. Some have a rhyming pattern. Others are purely in free verse.

Vatsala Radhakeesoon * *Depth of the River*

Also By
Vatsala Radhakeesoon

When Solitude Speaks

Vatsala Radhakeesoon * *Depth of the River*

www.ingramcontent.com/pod-product-compliance
Lightning Source LLC
Chambersburg PA
CBHW070150080526
44586CB00015B/1923